SUPER BOWL CHAMPIONS
NEW YORK JETS

WIDE RECEIVER
SANTONIO HOLMES

SUPER BOWL CHAMPIONS
NEW YORK JETS

AARON FRISCH

CREATIVE EDUCATION

Published by Creative Education
P.O. Box 227, Mankato, Minnesota 56002
Creative Education is an imprint of The Creative Company
www.thecreativecompany.us

Design and production by Blue Design
Art direction by Rita Marshall
Printed in the United States of America

Photographs by Getty Images (Al Bello, Scott Boehm,
Rob Carr, James Drake/Sports Illustrated, David Drapkin,
Focus on Sport, Nick Laham, Jim McIsaac, Vic Milton,
NFL Photos, Darryl Norenberg/NFL, Al Pereira/New
York Jets, Rich Schultz, Rick Stewart, Lou Witt/NFL, Jeff
Zelevansky)

Library of Congress Cataloging-in-Publication Data
Frisch, Aaron.
New York Jets / Aaron Frisch.
p. cm. — (Super bowl champions)
Includes index.
Summary: An elementary look at the New York Jets
professional football team, including its formation in 1960,
most memorable players, Super Bowl championship, and
stars of today.
ISBN 978-1-60818-383-8
1. New York Jets (Football team)—History—Juvenile
literature. I. Title.

GV956.N37F753 2014
796.332'64097471—dc23   2013014832

First Edition
9 8 7 6 5 4 3 2 1

DEFENSIVE TACKLE
SIONE POUHA

DON MAYNARD / 1960–72

Don was one of the first Jets stars. He was a receiver who caught a lot of Joe Namath's passes.

TABLE OF CONTENTS

MATT SNELL / 1964–72

Matt was a tough running back. He scored a touchdown to help the Jets win Super Bowl III.

TITANS AND JETS

In 1960, New York got a football team called the Titans. (A titan is a huge creature like a giant.) Three years later, the Titans became the Jets. The Jets have been flying ever since!

JOE KLECKO / 1977–87

Joe was a defensive tackle. He teamed up with Mark Gastineau to make many quarterback **sacks**.

Marriott
MARQUIS
Canon
HOWARD
Johnson's
Restaurants
cocktails
HOWARD JOHNSON'S
COCKTAILS
RESTAURANT
MARQUIS
MARQUIS

WELCOME TO NEW YORK

New York is a huge city in the state of New York. Close by is MetLife Stadium. It is the home of two New York football teams: the Jets and the Giants.

WAYNE CHREBET / 1995–2005

Wayne was a small but scrappy wide receiver. He played in New York for 11 seasons.

SOUND IT OUT

CHREBET: *kreh-BET*

A FAMOUS UPSET

The New York Jets are famous for a big **upset** in 1968. They played the Baltimore Colts in the Super Bowl. Almost everyone thought the Colts would win. But the Jets won 16–7!

12

SUPER BOWL III

"First, I prepare.
Then I have faith."
— JOE NAMATH

THE JETS' STORY

When the Jets were called the Titans, they played in the American Football League (AFL). The Titans lost a lot of games.

The team got better when it added quarterback Joe Namath. Joe promised that his team would win Super Bowl III (3). And it did!

TITANS VS. OILERS

MARK GASTINEAU

The Jets joined the National Football League (NFL) in 1970. They were not very good until they added players like defensive end Mark Gastineau in the 1980s.

KEVIN MAWAE / 1998–2005
Kevin was a star center. He played in the **Pro Bowl** every year from 1999 to 2004.

SOUND IT OUT

MAWAE: *muh-WY*

17

"At my eulogy, I don't want my daughter to talk about how many yards I rushed for. I want her to talk about the kind of man I was."
—CURTIS MARTIN

18

REX RYAN

Running back Curtis Martin helped New York win a lot of games in the 2000s. Curtis was the top running back in the NFL in 2004.

Rex Ryan became the Jets' coach in 2009. In 2009 and 2010, the Jets missed going to the Super Bowl by just one **playoff** game.

MARK SANCHEZ

2009–present

Mark joined the Jets in 2009. Fans hoped he would become the next great New York quarterback.

By 2013, D'Brickashaw Ferguson was one of the strongest tacklers in the league. New York fans hoped that he and the rest of the offense would help the Jets fly back to a Super Bowl soon!

D'BRICKASHAW FERGUSON

FACTS FILE

CONFERENCE/DIVISION:
American Football
Conference, East Division

TEAM COLORS:
Green and white

HOME STADIUM:
MetLife Stadium

SUPER BOWL VICTORY:
III, January 12, 1969
  16–7 over Baltimore
  Colts

NFL WEBSITE FOR KIDS:
http://nflrush.com

CORNERBACK
DARRELLE REVIS

GLOSSARY

playoff — one of the games that the best teams play after a season to see who the champion will be

Pro Bowl — a special game after the season that only the best NFL players get to play

sacks — plays in which a defensive player tackles a quarterback who is trying to throw a pass

upset — a game in which the team that most people think will win ends up losing

INDEX